ENGLISH GRAMMAR AND VOCABULARY

This exercise book is for students of English as a foreign language who have completed level A1 and A2. The exercises are a suitable revision for anyone studying for the KET or PET exam.

If you are at a low level in your English language learning, then it is of utmost importance to revise what you learned on your last English course, or, if you are attending an elementary English course, revise what you are learning.

As a beginner, it is all too easy to forget what you learned if you do not revise on a regular basis. If you go for a tennis lesson, you need to find time to practise what you learned before your tennis coach begins the second lesson After the second lesson you need to practise what you did at lesson one and lesson two. It is the same when learning anything and English is no exception. These exercises are compiled to help beginners revise before moving to pre intermediate level.

The lower your level is, the more practice you will need. Practice makes perfect. The more you practice the easier English will become.

There are easily accessible answers after each exercise.

English Grammar Exercises For Elementary Students

Exercise One

Verb 'To Be' Simple Present Tense

Fill in the gaps with the negative and the question forms of the following affirmations. An example is given. Use contracted forms for the negatives.

Example:

0. I 'm English/**I'm not English/Am I English**?
1. John's German/he ______/_____?
2. My grandparents are French/they ______/_____?
3. Paul's sister's married/she ______/_____?
4. My dog's white/it ______/_____?
5. Jane and Lucy are sisters/they ______/_____?
6. Mother and I are late/we ______/_____?
7. The postman's here/he ______/_____?
8. Jenny's in the kitchen/she ______/_____?
9. Janet's on the train/she ______/_____?
10. It's very cold today/it ______/_____?

Exercise One/Answers

1. John's German. He isn't German. Is he German?
2. My grandparents are French. They aren't French. Are they French?
3. Paul's sister's married. She isn't married. Is she married?
4. My dog's white. It isn't white. Is it white?
5. Jane and Lucy are sisters. They aren't sisters. Are they sisters?
6. Mother and I are late. We aren't late. Are we late?
7. The postman's here. He isn't here. Is he here?
8. Jenny's in the kitchen. She isn't in the kitchen. Is she in the kitchen?
9. Janet's on the train. She isn't on the train. Is she on the train?
10. It's very cold today. It isn't very cold today. Is it very cold today?

Exercise Two

Long Forms of the verb 'be'

Change the contracted forms to the long forms of the verb 'be'. Look at the example.

Example:

0. He's from Sweden. He's Swedish/He **is** from Sweden. He **is** Swedish.
1. Henriette's from Germany. She's German. ______/_____.
2. He's my brother. He isn't my friend. ______/_____.
3. His sister's married. She isn't single. ______/_____.
4. Snow's white. It isn't black. ______/_____.
5. The sun's yellow. It isn't green. ______/_____.
6. That new restaurant's expensive. It isn't cheap. ______/_____.
7. The dog's lively. It isn't quiet. ______/_____.
8. The winter in Canada's cold. It isn't warm. ______/_____.
9. I'm Sally. I'm not Jane. ______/_____.
10. They're my parents. They aren't my neighbours. ______/_____.
11. We're late. We aren't early. ______/_____.
12. They aren't old. They're young. ______/_____.
13. Mike's in Switzerland. He isn't in Spain. ______/_____.
14. Mother's in the kitchen. She isn't in the bedroom. ______/_____.
15. They're not your books. They're mine. ______/_____.

16. The sky's blue. It isn't red. ______/_____.

17. English isn't easy. It's difficult. ______/_____.

18. My brothers aren't lawyers. They're doctors. ______/_____.

19. We aren't enemies. We're friends. ______/_____.

20. She's not on holiday. She's at work. ______/_____.

Exercise Two/Answers

1. Henriette's from Germany. She's German. Henriette **is** from Germany. She **is** German.
2. He's my brother. He isn't my friend. He **is** my brother. He **is not** my friend.
3. His sister's married. She isn't single. His sister **is** married. She **is not** single.
4. Snow's white. It isn't black. Snow **is** white. It **is not** black.
5. The sun's yellow. It isn't green. The sun **is** yellow. It **is not** green
6. That new restaurant's expensive. It isn't cheap. That new restaurant **is** expensive. It **is not** cheap.
7. The dog's lively. It isn't quiet. The dog **is** lively. It **is not** quiet.
8. The winter in Canada's cold. It isn't warm. The winter in Canada **is** cold. It **is not** warm.
9. I'm Sally. I'm not Jane. I **am** Sally. I **am not** Jane.

10. They're my parents. They aren't my neighbours. They **are** my parents. They **are not** my neighbours.

11. We're late. We aren't early. We **are** late. We **are not** early.

12. They aren't old. They're young. They **are not** old. They **are** young.

13. Mike's in Switzerland. He isn't in Spain. Mike **is** in Switzerland. He **is not** in Spain.

14. Mother's in the kitchen. She isn't in the bedroom. Mother **is** in the kitchen. She **is not** in the bedroom.

15. They're not your books. They're mine. They **are not** your books. They **are** mine.

16. The sky's blue. It isn't red. The sky **is** blue. It **is not** red.

17. English isn't easy. It's difficult. English **is not** easy. It **is** difficult.

18. My brothers aren't lawyers. They're doctors. My brothers **are not** lawyers. They **are** doctors.

19. We aren't enemies. We're friends. We **are not** enemies. We **are** friends.

20. She's not on holiday. She's at work. She **is not** on holiday. She **is** at work.

Exercise Three/Part One

Replace the nouns with subject pronouns. First look at the example.

Example:

0. How is your mother? How is **she**?
1. How are your parents? How are ___?
2. How old is your brother. How old is ___?
3. How old is Jenny? How old is ___?
4. How old are your grandparents? How old are ___?
5. Where is my bag? Where is ___?
6. Where are my glasses? Where are ___?
7. Why is Paul here? Why is ___ here?
8. Why are Jean and Alan late? Why are ___ late?
9. When's your birthday? When is ___?
10. What's in this box? What's in ___?

Exercise Three/Answers/Part One

1. How are your parents? How are **they**?

2. How old is your brother. How old is **he**?

3. How old is Jenny? How old is **she**?

4. How old are your grandparents? How old are **they**?

5. Where is my bag? Where is **it**?

6. Where are my glasses? Where are **they**?

7. Why is Paul here? Why is **he** here?

8. Why are Jean and Alan late? Why are **they** late?

9. When's your birthday? When is **it**?

10. What's in this box? What's in **it**?

Exercise Three/Part Two

Match the above questions with an Answer from A - H

A. Seventy nine and eighty four

B. Because there was a traffic jam

C. He's twenty six

D. They're not so bad thanks

E. A birthday present for my aunt Jenny

F. To speak to my brother

G. I don't know. About twenty two

H. They're on top of the fridge

I. It's on the chair in the kitchen

J. It's on 1st September

EXERCISE THREE/PART/TWO/ANSWERS

1.d 2.c 3.g 4.a 5.i 6.h 7.f 8.b 9.j 10.e

Exercise Four

Verb 'Be' or Possessive

Read the following text. Which **'s**. indicates the contracted form of 'is' and which indicates the possessive. Mark with a **B** if it is a form of the verb 'be',or mark with a **P**, if it is the possessive.

Example:

Mary's brother's a doctor.

0. Mary's brother = the brother of Mary. This is the possessive so you mark with a **P**. He's a doctor = He is a doctor so you mark with a **B**

1. Patricia's husband's an accountant.
2. He's a tall man with dark hair.
3. John's pen is on the desk.
4. Jane's brother's at home at the moment.
5. He's asleep.
6. Janet's not here. She's out at the moment.
7. Mark's on holiday.
8. Simon's dog is dark brown.
9. Sally's at work.
10. Frederick's mother's in the kitchen.

Exercise Four/Answers

1. Patricia's husband's an accountant. Patricia's **P** husband is **B**

2. He's a tall man with dark hair. He is **B**

3. John's pen is on the desk. John's pen **P**

4. Jane's brother's at home at the moment. Jane's **P** brother is **B**

5. He's asleep. He is **B**

6. Janet's not here. She's out at the moment. Janet is **B** She is **B**

7. Mark's on holiday. Mark is **B**

8. Simon's dog is dark brown. Simon's **P** dog

9. Sally's at work. Sally is **B**

10. Frederick's mother's in the kitchen. Frederick's **P** Mother is **B**

Exercise Five

Possessive Pronouns

Replace the following with one of the following possessive pronouns: *his, her, its, our, their*

Example:

0. Mary's brother. **Her** brother.

1. Peter's dog. ___ dog.

2. Mother and father's car. ___ car.

3. Julie's boyfriend. ___ boyfriend.

4. The dog's bone. ___ bone.

5. It's my house and it's your house. It's ___ house.

6. Peter's sister's house is beautiful. ___ house is beautiful.

7. The boys' ball. ___ ball.

8. The girls' dolls. ___ dolls.

9. Sally's brother. ___ brother.

10. Molly and John's bikes are new. ___ bikes are new.

Exercise Five/Answers

1. Peter's dog. **His** dog.

2. Mother and father's car. **Their** car.

3. Julie's boyfriend. **Her** boyfriend.

4. The dog's bone. **Its** bone.

5. It's my house and it's your house. It's **our** house.

6. Peter's sister's house is beautiful. **Her** house is beautiful.

7. The boys' ball. **Their** ball.

8. The girls' dolls. **Their** dolls.

9. Sally's brother. **Her** brother.

10. Molly and John's bikes are new. **Their** bikes are new.

Remember that the apostrophe moves when the noun is plural.

Example:

The girl's dolls. The dolls of one girl.

The girls' dolls. The dolls of more than one girl.

EXERCISE SIX

POSSESSIVE PRONOUNS WITHOUT THE NOUN

Example:

0. It's my bag. It's **mine**.

1. It's Peter's dog. It's ___

2. It's mother and father's car It's ___

3. They're Julie's books. They're ___

4. It's the dog's bone. It's ___

5. It's my house and it's your house. It's ___

6. It's Joan and Lily's radio. It's ___

7. It's the boys' ball. It's ___

8. They're the girls' dolls. They're ___

9. They're John's trousers. They're ___

10. They're Molly and John's new bikes. They're___

EXERCISE SIX/ANSWERS

1. It's Peter's dog. It's **his**.

2. It's mother and father's car It's **theirs**.

3. They're Julie's books. They're **hers**.

4. It's the dog's bone. It's **its**.

5. It's my house and it's your house. It's **ours**.

6. It's Joan and Lily's radio. It's **theirs**.

7. It's the boys' ball. It's **theirs**.

8. They're the girls' dolls. They're **theirs**.

9. They're John's trousers. They're **his.**

10. They're Molly and John's new bikes. They're **theirs**.

Exercise Seven

Write questions with '**WHOSE**' for the following answers from Exercise Six.

Remember: we use My, your, his, her, its, our and their + noun.. We use mine, yours, his, hers, its, ours and theirs. without the noun. Usually because the noun is already used in the question so there is no need to repeat it.

WHOSE pronunciation /hu:z/

Example:

0. **Whose is that bag**?

It's my bag/it's mine

1. It's Peter's dog. It's his dog/it's his.
2. It's mother and father's car It's their car/it's theirs.
3. They're Julie's books. They're her books/they're hers.
4. It's the dog's bone. It's its bone/it's its.
5. It's my house and it's your house. It's our house/it's ours.
6. It's Joan and Lily's radio. It's their radio/it's theirs.
7. It's the boys' ball. It's their ball/it's theirs.
8. They're the girls' dolls. They're their dolls/they're theirs.
9. They're John's trousers. They're his trousers/they're his.
10. They're Molly and John's new bikes. They're their bikes/they're theirs.

EXERCISE SEVEN/ANSWERS

Whose is that dog?

1. It's Peter's dog. It's his dog/it's his.

Whose is that car?

2. It's mother and father's car It's their car/it's theirs.

Whose are those books?

3. They're Julie's books. They're her books/their hers.

Whose is that bone?

4. It's the dog's bone. It's its bone/it's its.

Whose is that house?

5. It's my house and it's your house. It's our house/it's ours.

Whose is that radio?

6. It's Joan and Lily's radio. It's their radio/it's theirs.

Whose is that ball?

7. It's the boys' ball. It's their ball/it's theirs.

Whose are those dolls?

8. They're the girls' dolls. They're their dolls/they're theirs.

Whose are those trousers?

9. They're John's trousers. They're his trousers/they're his.

Whose are those new bikes?

10. They're Molly and John's new bikes. They're their bikes/they're theirs.

Note from the author:

There is a variation to the question with '**whose**'

Example:

Whose is that car?

Whose car is that?

Whose are those trousers?

Whose trousers are those?

Note to remember

If the object is in front of you, you say: Whose is THIS car? If it is at a distance, you say: Whose is THAT car?

In the plural form, if the object is in front of you, you say: Whose are THESE trousers? If the object is at a distance, and you can see it, then you say: Whose are THOSE trousers?

Exercise Eight

The Present Continuous

Now do the following exercise. There is an example to illustrate what you should do. Make the negative and the questions using the short forms of the verb 'be'.

Example:

0. I 'm reading/**I'm not reading/Am I reading**?
1. Jill's sleeping/she ______/_____?
2. My cousins are eating/they ______/_____?
3. Mike's brother's sitting on the sofa/he ______/_____?
4. My cat's playing with a ball of wool/it ______/_____?
5. Henry and Linda are talking/they ______/_____?
6. Father and I are watching TV/we ______/_____?
7. The gardener's cutting the grass/he ______/_____?
8. Mandy's having a shower/she ______/_____
9. Steve's cycling/he ______/_____?
10. The boy's getting dressed/he ______/_____?

Exercise Eight/Answers

1. Jill's sleeping. She isn't sleeping. Is she sleeping?

2. My cousins are eating. They aren't eating. Are they eating?

3. Mike's brother's sitting on the sofa. He isn't sleeping on the sofa. Is he sleeping on the sofa?

4. My cat's playing with a ball of wool. It isn't playing with a ball of wool. Is it playing with a ball of wool?

5. Henry and Linda are talking. They aren't talking. Are they talking?

6. Father and I are watching TV. We aren't watching TV. Are we watching TV?

7. The gardener's cutting the grass. He isn't cutting the grass. Is he cutting the grass?

8. Mandy's having a shower. She isn't having a shower. Is she having a shower?

9. Steve's cycling. He isn't cycling. Is he cycling?

10. The boy's getting dressed. He isn't getting dressed. Is he getting dressed?

Exercise Nine

Present Simple/Affirmatives/Questions and Negatives

Example:

0. I **live** in London/I **don't live** in London/**Do** I **live** in London?
1. Jennifer loves chocolate/she ______/_____?
2. My friends speak English/they ______/_____?
3. Mary's sister drinks water every day/she ______/_____?
4. My cat plays a lot/it ______/_____?
5. Mark and his brother share a room /they ______/_____?
6. Peter and I work for the same company/we ______/_____?
7. Mother cooks every day/she ______/_____?
8. John works in the city centre/he ______/_____?
9. Raymond has milk and coffee for breakfast/he ______/_____?
10. My car works really well/it ______/_____?

Exercise Nine/Answers

1. Jennifer loves chocolate. She **doesn't love** chocolate. **Does** she **love** chocolate?
2. My friends speak English. They **don't speak** English. **Do** they **speak** English?

3. Mary's sister drinks water every day. She **doesn't drink** water every day. **Does** she **drink** water every day?

4. My cat plays a lot. It **doesn't play** a lot. **Does** it **play** a lot?

5. Mark and his brother share a room. They **don't share** a room. **Do** they **share** a room?

6. Peter and I work for the same company. We **don't work** for the same company. **Do** we **work** for the same company?

7. Mother cooks every day. She **doesn't cook** every day. **Does** she **cook** every day?

8. John works in the city centre. He **doesn't work** in the city centre. **Does** he **work** in the city centre?

9. Raymond has milk and coffee for breakfast. He **doesn't have** milk and coffee for breakfast. **Does** he **have** milk and coffee for breakfast?

10. My car works really well. It **doesn't work** really well. **Does** it **work** really well?

Exercise Ten

Adverbs of Frequency

Adverbs of frequency are used mainly with the present simple tense. They show how frequent something occurs.

Put the following adverbs of frequency in the correct position in each sentence

Example:

0. I **never** have breakfast. (never)

1. Simon gets up early. (often)
2. We arrive on time for class. We are late. (always/never)
3. The teacher is happy because we do our homework. (always x 2)
4. My sisters argue with my mother about nothing. (often)
5. We go to the cinema. (hardly ever)
6. John sleeps until lunchtime on Sundays. (sometimes)
7. The children are naughty. (often)
8. They have cereal with milk before they go to school. (usually)
9. It is hot in Spain in August. (always)
10. Are they so well behaved? (always)

Exercise Ten/Answers

Adverbs of frequency come *before* the main verb between the subject and verb. and *after* the verb 'be'. The adverb of frequency '**sometimes**' is an exception. It can go *before* the main verb, *before* the subject, or *after* the main verb. With the verb 'be' it cannot come before the verb but it can come before the subject.

Example:

Sometimes I go home early.

I **sometimes** go home early.

I go home early **sometimes**.

Sometimes I am late.

I am **sometimes** late.

I am late **sometimes**.

1. Simon **often** gets up early.
2. We **always** arrive on time for class. We are **never** late.
3. The teacher is **always** happy because we **always** do our homework.
4. My sisters **often** argue with my mother about nothing.
5. We **hardly ever** go to the cinema.
6. **Sometimes** John sleeps until lunchtime on Sundays.

   John **sometimes** sleeps until lunchtime on Sundays.
7. The children are **often** naughty.
8. They **usually** have cereal with milk before they go to school.

9. It is **always** hot in Spain in August.

10. Are they **always** *so well behaved?

*They are **always** naughty. **After** the verb ‘be’.. The subject and the verb are inverted in the question.

Exercise Eleven

The past tense of the verb 'to be'

Put the verb 'be' into the past tense:

(A) = Affirmative **(N)** = Negative and **(Q)** = Question

Example:

0. We **were** late for the lesson yesterday so the teacher **was** angry. **(A)**

1. I _________ top of the class when I _________ only ten years old. **(A)**

2. We _________ in London in 2010 for a holiday. **(A)**

3. My son _________ ill yesterday. **(A)**

4. My brothers ______________ at home at lunchtime. **(N)**

5. There _________ no lessons yesterday because the teachers _________ on strike. **(A)**

6. _________ Pamela in your class last year? **Q**

7. He _________ very nice to me this morning. **(N)** He _________ very nasty. **(A)**

8. That meat _________ delicious. I would like some more. **(A)**

9. It _________ a very hot day yesterday. **(A)**

10. It _________ cold yesterday. **(N)**

Exercise Eleven/Answers

(A) = Affirmative **(N)** = Negative and **(Q)** = Question

1. I **was** top of the class when I **was** only ten years old. **(A)**

2. We **were** in London in 2010 for a holiday. **(A)**

3. My son **was** ill yesterday. **(A)**

4. My brothers **weren't** at home at lunchtime. **(N)**

5. There **were** no lessons yesterday because the teachers **were** on strike.

(A)

6. **Was** Pamela in your class last year? **(Q)**

7. He **wasn't** very nice to me this morning. **(N)** He **was** very nasty. **(A)**

8. That meat **was** delicious. I would like some more. **(A)**

9. It **was** a very hot day yesterday. **(A)**

10. It **wasn't** cold yesterday. **(N)**

Exercise Twelve

Past Tense of Verbs/Questions/Negatives/Affirmatives

Use the verb in brackets in the affirmative, negative or question form.

Example:

0. We **didn't go** to the lake. We **went** to the beach. (NOT GO) (GO)

1. I _________ a lot of money when I _________ on holiday last week. **(**SPEND) (BE)

2. I _________ £200 on the lottery. I _________ a new digital camera with the money. **(**WIN) (BUY)

3. My daughter _________ the house early this morning. (LEAVE)

4. The girls _________ English when we _________ in England last summer.(SPEAK) (BE)

5. I_____________ too much yesterday. I _________ ill all day. (EAT) (FEEL)

6. _________ you _________ home late last night? **(**COME)

7. He _________ to me this morning. He _________ he _________ time. (NOT SPEAK) (SAY) (NOT HAVE)

8. That meat _________ delicious. Can I have some more? (BE)

9. It _________ a very hot day yesterday. (BE)

10. It _________ cold yesterday. (NOT BE)

EXERCISE TWELVE/ANSWERS

1. I **spent** a lot of money when I **was** on holiday last week.

2. I **won** £200 on the lottery. I **bought** a new digital camera with the money.

3. My daughter **left** the house early this morning.

4. The girls **spoke** English when we **were** in England last summer.

5. I **ate** too much yesterday. I **felt** ill all day.

6. **Did** you **come** home late last night?

7. He **didn't speak** to me this morning. He **said** he **didn't have** time.

8. That meat **was** delicious. Can I have some more? BE.

9. It **was** a very hot day yesterday.BE.

10. It **wasn't** cold yesterday. NOT BE.

Exercise Thirteen

Question Words

Put one of the following question words in the gaps below. Look first at the answers and then decide on the question.

WHEN-WHY-WHICH-WHAT-WHERE-WHO-HOW-HOW OLD-HOW MUCH-HOW MANY-HOW OFTEN

Example:

0. I was happy because he came to my party.

Why were you happy?

1. I bought some cheese.

_____ did you buy at the supermarket today?

2. I saw Michael.

_____ did you see this morning?

3. We went on a picnic.

_____ did you do last Sunday?

4. He's twenty two.

_____ is John?

5. Because I ate too much

_____ did you feel so ill?

6. It's on 23rd May.

_____ is your birthday?

7. Just a little please.

_____ milk do you want in your coffee?

8. Just one, thanks.

_____ biscuits do you want?

9. The blue one

_____ pen do you want? The red one or the blue one.

10. Jane

_____ is your name?

11. Much better.

_____ do you feel today?

12. He's talking on the phone.

_____ is Stephen doing?

13. Near the park in Crimson Road.

_____ is your new house?

14. I watch TV.

_____ do you usually do after dinner?

15. They're at the cinema.

_____ are your parents this evening?

16. It's red.

_____ colour is your new car?

17. I had a cheese and onion pie.

_____ did you have for dinner last night?

18. He's outside washing his car.

_____ is your brother?

19. Twice a week.

_____ do you wash your hair?

20. In France.

_____ does your brother live?

EXERCISE THIRTEEN/ANSWERS

1. I bought some cheese.

What did you buy at the supermarket today?

2. I saw Michael.

Who did you see this morning?

3. We went on a picnic.

Where did you do last Sunday?

4. He's twenty two.

How old is John?

5. Because I ate too much

Why did you feel so ill?

6. It's on 23rd May.

When is your birthday?

7. Just a little please.

How much milk do you want in your coffee?

8. Just one, thanks.

How many biscuits do you want?

9. The blue one

Which pen do you want? The red one or the blue one.

10. Jane

What is your name?

11. Much better.

How do you feel today?

12. He's talking on the phone.

What is Stephen doing?

13. Near the park in Crimson Road.

Where is your new house?

14. I watch TV.

What do you usually do after dinner?

15. They're at the cinema.

Where are your parents this evening?

16. It's red.

What colour is your new car?

17. I had a cheese and onion pie.

What did you have for dinner last night?

18. He's outside washing his car.

Where is your brother?

19. Twice a week.

How often do you wash your hair?

20. In France.

Where does your brother live?

Exercise Fourteen

Short Answers

Use a short answer in response to the following questions.

Example:

0. Do you speak English? **Yes I do**

1. Is John your father? No _____.
2. Do you like your job? No _____.
3. Is the sun cold? No _____.
4. Were you at work yesterday? Yes _____.
5. Does Mary live near you? Yes _____.
6. Is it your birthday tomorrow? No _____.
7. Does your mother like the present you gave her for Christmas? Yes _____.
8. Did you see Mark when you were out this morning? No _____.
9. Was your new watch expensive? Yes _____.
10. Do they speak French? Yes _____.
11. Is that book you're reading good? Yes _____.
12. Did you go to the bank today? No _____.
13. Does he live in this area? Yes _____.
14. Did you watch that great film that was on TV last night? No _____.
15. Was she happy to see you again? No _____.
16. Are these books yours? No _____.

17. Is he in the shower? Yes _____.

18. Did they thank you for the present? Yes _____.

19. Is your cat white? Yes _____.

20. Are we late? Yes _____.

EXERCISE FOURTEEN/ANSWERS

1. Is John your father? No **he isn't**.

2. Do you like your job? No **No I don't**.

3. Is the sun cold? No **it isn't**.

4. Were you at work yesterday? Yes **I was**.

5. Does Mary live near you? Yes **she does**.

6. Is it your birthday tomorrow? No **it isn't**.

7. Does your mother like the present you gave her for Christmas? Yes **she does**.

8. Did you see Mark when you were out this morning? No **I didn't**.

9. Was your new watch expensive? Yes **it was**.

10. Do they speak French? Yes **they do**.

11. Is that book you're reading good? Yes **it is**.

12. Did you go to the bank today? No **I didn't**.

13. Does he live in this area? Yes **he does**.

14. Did you watch that great film that was on TV last night? No **I didn't**.

15. Was she happy to see you again? No **<u>she wasn't</u>**.

16. Are these books yours? No **<u>they aren't</u>**.

17. Is he in the shower? Yes **<u>he is</u>**.

18. Did they thank you for the present? Yes **<u>they did</u>**.

19. Is your cat white? Yes **<u>it is</u>**.

20. Are we late? Yes **<u>we are</u>**.

Note from the author:

When the question begins with an auxiliary verb, we normally reply with the short answer, using the same auxiliary verb which was used in the question. When a question word precedes the auxiliary verb, then we cannot reply with a short answer. We need to give a full answer:

Example:

<u>Do</u> you live in France? Yes I **<u>do</u>**

Where **<u>do</u>** you **<u>live</u>**? **<u>I live</u>** in France

Exercise Fifteen

Subject Pronouns

Replace the **underlined** nouns with subject pronouns to make the text sound more natural

Example:

My sister lives in London. **My sister** is a doctor. She has a dog. **The dog** is a big dog.

My sister lives in London. **She** is a doctor. She has a dog. **It** is a big dog.

Mandy Sweeney lives in a large house. **The large house** is in Edinburgh in Scotland. **Mandy** lives with her husband and their two children. **Her husband and their two children** help Mandy to clean the house. Mandy is a fanatic for cleaning. **Mandy** is only happy when the house is clean. **Mandy and her husband and their two children** also have a large garden. **The garden** is full of flowers because Mandy loves gardening.

Exercise Fifteen/Answers

Mandy Sweeney lives in a large house. **It** is in Edinburgh in Scotland. **She** lives with her husband and their two children. **They** help Mandy to clean the house. Mandy is a fanatic for cleaning. **She** is only happy when the house is clean. **They** also have a large garden. **It** is full of flowers because Mandy loves gardening.

EXERCISE SIXTEEN

OBJECT PRONOUNS

Example:

0. This book is very good. Do you want to read **it**?

1. Your sister is very nice. I really like _____.

2. This milk is not fresh. Don't drink _____. Throw _____.out.

3. I love your new shoes. Where did you buy _____?

4. "Can I have your homework please", said the teacher? "Sorry Miss Jones, I forgot to do _____."

5. I don't have any money to buy lunch today. I left _____ at home.

6. Boy:"Where are my pyjamas?" Mother: "I left _____ on top o f your bed."

7. Janet:"This is my brother Paul." Alan:"I know. I remember _____. We went to the same primary school when we were young boys."

8. Where are my keys? I left _____ on the kitchen table but they're not there anymore.

9. Mary:"This bag is very heavy." John:"Don't worry. I'll carry _____. for you."

10. David:"Where's the postman? He's late today. I'm expecting a parcel from my aunt in America." Jane:"I saw _____ in the next street about five minutes ago. He should be here soon."

11. Mary:"My hair is very greasy today." Mother:"Well why don't you wash _____.then?"

12. Fred:"The last time I saw Jeff and Matilda was about six months ago." Peter:"I saw _____. in the shopping mall last Saturday."

13. Mary:"I bought a new dress for the party while I was out this morning. Do you like _____.?" Sally:"Yes, I love _____. It's a really nice colour."

14. Steve: "Did you read the newspaper this morning?" Patricia:"No, I didn't. Where is _____.? I'll read it once I finish drying my hair."

15. I can't find my glasses. I'm sure I left _____. on the bedside cabinet but they're not there.

16. There are no biscuits left. Who ate _____ all?

17. Jack: "Where's my jacket?" Mother: "I hung _____ up in the wardrobe."

18. Peter: "What wonderful photographs." Edward: "I know. I took _____ with my new camera."

19. My brother and I are very lucky. Our parents bought _____ a new top of the range computer.

20. Oh look! There's Tom and Jill. Can you see _____? I don't think they can see _____.

Exercise Sixteen/Answers

1. Your sister is very nice. I really like **her**.

2. This milk is not fresh. Don't drink **it**. Throw **it** out.

3. I love your new shoes. Where did you buy **them**?

4. "Can I have your homework please", said the teacher? "Sorry Miss Jones, I forgot to do **it**."

5. I don't have any money to buy lunch today. I left **it** at home.

6. Boy:"Where are my pyjamas?" Mother: "I left **them** on top of your bed."

7. Janet:"This is my brother Paul." Alan:"I know. I remember **him**. We went to the same primary school when we were young boys."

8. Where are my keys? I left **them** on the kitchen table but they're not there anymore.

9. Mary:"This bag is very heavy." John:"Don't worry. I'll carry **it** for you."

10. David:"Where's the postman? He's late today. I'm expecting a parcel from my aunt in America." Jane:"I saw **him** in the next street about five minutes ago. He should be here soon."

11. Mary:"My hair is very greasy today." Mother:"Well why don't you wash **it** then?"

12. Fred:"The last time I saw Jeff and Matilda was about six months ago." Peter:"I saw **them** in the shopping mall last Saturday."

13. Mary:"I bought a new dress for the party while I was out this morning. Do you like **it**?" Sally:"Yes, I love **it.** It's a really nice colour."

14. Steve: "Did you read the newspaper this morning?" Patricia:"No, I didn't. Where is **it**? I'll read it once I finish drying my hair."

15. I can't find my glasses. I'm sure I left **them** on the bedside cabinet but they're not there.

16. There are no biscuits left. Who ate **them** all?

17. Jack: "Where's my jacket?" Mother: "I hung **it** up in the wardrobe."

18. Peter: "What wonderful photographs." Edward: "I know. I took **them** with my new camera."

19. My brother and I are very lucky. Our parents bought **us** a new top of the range computer.

20. Oh look! There's Tom and Jill. Can you see **them**? I don't think they can see **us**.

Exercise Seventeen

Rewrite the following sentences using the long forms of the auxiliary verb 'dodoes/did' in their negative forms.

Example:

0. I didn't know his name was Mike I **did not** know his name was Mike.

1. He doesn't speak English but he speaks Spanish, German and Japanese.
2. I didn't see you on the bus this morning. Where were you?
3. Didn't he tell you he was married?
4. Don't open the window. It's very cold outside.
5. They don't live in England anymore. They immigrated to Canada last year.
6. Paul doesn't want to eat. He doesn't feel well.
7. They didn't like the meal so they didn't finish it.
8. You don't know me but I know you, said the voice on the telephone.
9. My parents didn't meet until they were 38 years old.
10. Don't you want to come with us?

<u>Exercise Seventeen/Answers</u>

1. He **<u>does not</u>** speak English but he speaks Spanish, German and Japanese.
2. I **<u>did not</u>** see you on the bus this morning. Where were you?
3. **<u>Did he not</u>** tell you he was married?
4. **<u>Do not</u>** open the window. It's very cold outside.
5. They **<u>do not</u>** live in England anymore. They immigrated to Canada last year.
6. Paul **<u>does not</u>** want to eat. He **<u>does not</u>** feel well.
7. They **<u>did not</u>** like the meal so they **<u>did not</u>** finish it.
8. You **<u>do not</u>** know me but I know you, said the voice on the telephone.
9. My parents **<u>did not</u>** meet until they were 38 years old.
10. **<u>Do you not</u>** want to come with us?

Exercise Eighteen

Put the opposites of the following underlined adjectives into the gaps.

Example:

0. Jane is **thin**. She only weighs 55 kilos. John is **fat**. He weighs 120 kilos.

1. English is easy. Japanese is _____.
2. Today it is hot. Yesterday it was _____.
3. My dog is black. John's dog is_____.
4. My sister is young. My grandmother is _____,
5. This chair is hard. The other one is _____.
6. Jill's hair is long. My hair is _____.
7. My brother is tall. I am _____.
8. That shelf is high. The other one is _____.
9. The street where I live is narrow. The main road is _____.
10. The public transport in London is expensive, but in Rome it is _____.

Exercise Eighteen/Answers

1. English is easy. Japanese is **difficult**.
2. Today it is hot. Yesterday it was **cold**.
3. My dog is black. John's dog is **white**.
4. My sister is young. My grandmother is **old**.
5. This chair is hard. The other one is **soft**.
6. Jill's hair is long. My hair is **short**.
7. My brother is tall. I am **short**.
8. That shelf is high. The other one is **low**.
9. The street where I live is narrow. The main road is **wide**.
10. The public transport in London is expensive, but in Rome it is **cheap**.

EXERCISE NINETEEN/PART ONE

THERE IS/THERE ARE

Rewrite the following sentences using the long forms of the auxiliary verb 'dodoes/did' in their negative forms.

Example:

0. There ____ a bank on the corner of my street. There **<u>is</u>** a bank on the corner of my street.

1. There ____ three supermarkets in the area where I live.

2. There ____ two fruit shops. One in the Main Street and the other in a side street.

3. There ____ primary school next to the park.

4. There ____ also a post office. It's next to the bank.

5. There ____ a police station in the centre of town.

6. Opposite the police station there ____ a bakery.

7. Behind the bakery there ____ a car park.

8. Opposite the car park there ____ a fire station.

9. In the fire station there ____ many firemen.

10. Near the fire station there ____ a train station.

Exercise Nineteen/Answers/Part One

1. There **are** three supermarkets in the area where I live.

2. There **are** two fruit shops; one in the main street and the other in a side street.

3. There **is** a primary school next to the park.

4. There **is** also a post office. It's next to the bank.

5. There **is** a police station in the centre of town.

6. Opposite the police station there **is** a bakery.

7. Behind the bakery there **is** a car park.

8. Opposite the car park there **is** a fire station.

9. In the fire station there **are** many firemen.

10. Near the fire station there **is** a train station.

Exercise Nineteen/Part two

Make the following ten sentences negative and then make them into the question form

Example:

0. There are **some** people in the street. There **aren't any** people in the street

1. There are two boys in front of the school gates.

 ____

 ____

2. There are some girls watching the boys.

____

____

3. There is a cat sitting on a wall near the girls.

____

____

4. There are some children in the street.

____

____

5. There is a policeman near the children.

____

____

6. There are some photographers.

____

____

7. There are two police cars behind the photographers.

____

____

8. There are three women watching.

____

____

9. There is a dog barking at the cat.

____

____

10. There is a journalist taking notes.

____

____

Exercise Nineteen/Answers/Part Two

1. There **aren't any** boys in front of the school gates.

   Are there any boys in front of the school gates?

2. There **aren't any** girls watching the boys.

   Are there any girls watching the boys?

3. There **isn't a** cat sitting on a wall near the girls.

   Is there a cat sitting on the wall near the girls?

4. There **aren't any** children in the street.

   Are there any children in the street?

5. There **isn't a** policeman near the children.

   Is there a policeman near the children?

6. There **aren't any** photographers.

   Are there any photographers?

7. There **aren't any** police cars behind the photographers.

   Are there any police cars behind the photographers?

8. There **aren't any** women watching.

   Are there any women watching?

9. There **isn't a** dog barking at the cat.

   Is there a dog barking at the cat?

10. There **isn't a** journalist taking notes. Is there a journalist taking notes?

EXERCISE TWENTY

HOW MUCH/HOW MANY

Countable or Uncountable

Example:

0. ____ cheese do you want?

Answer: **How much**

1. ____ biscuits do you want with your tea?
2. ____ milk is there in the fridge?
3. ____ water do you want?
4. ____ rice do you want me to cook?
5. ____ eggs did you buy?
6. ____ fish do you eat?
7. ____ meat does John eat per day?
8. ____ money do you put in the bank?
9. ____ do you weigh?
10. ____ kilos do you weigh?
11. ____ children went to the party?
12. ____ ice cream did you eat?
13. ____ women work in your office?
14. ____ slices of bread did he eat?
15. ____ bread does she buy each day for her large family?

16. ____ apples did you pick from the tree?

17. ____ sugar do you take in your coffee?

18. ____ teaspoonfuls of sugar do you take in your tea?

19. ____ did you pay for your new phone?

20. ____ live in your building?

EXERCISE TWENTY/ANSWERS

1. **How many** biscuits do you want with your tea?
2. **How much** milk is there in the fridge?
3. **How much** water do you want?
4. **How much** rice do you want me to cook?
5. **How many** eggs did you buy?
6. **How much** fish do you eat?
7. **How much** meat does John eat per day?
8. **How much** money do you put in the bank?
9. **How much** do you weigh?
10. **How many** kilos do you weigh?
11. **How many** children went to the party?
12. **How much** ice cream did you eat?
13. **How many** women work in your office?
14. **How many** slices of bread did he eat?

15. **How much** bread does she buy each day for her large family?

16. **How many** apples did you pick from the tree?

17. **How much** sugar do you take in your coffee?

18. **How many** teaspoonfuls of sugar do you take in your tea?

19. **How much** did you pay for your new phone?

20. **How many** people live in your building?

Exercise Twenty One

Too/Too many/Too much

Fill the gaps with *too/too much/too many*

Example:

0. I drank ____ wine last night. Now I've got a terrible headache.

Answer: I drank **too much** wine last night. Now I've got a terrible headache.

1. The bus is crowded. There are ____ people on it.

2. Person A: "This jumper is ____ small." Person B: "Take it back and get a bigger one."

3. I went to the supermarket to buy some food. It was ____ late. When I got there, it was closed.

4. There were ____ people in the post office. I didn't have time to wait in the queue.

5. Person A: "This cake is disgusting. Person B: I know. I put ____ flour in it.

6. Person B: "I think you left it in the oven for ____ long. It's burnt around the edges."

7. I ate ____ for lunch today so I don't want any dinner. I'm not hungry.

8. That table is ____ big. There is no space in the kitchen. We need to buy a smaller one.

9. The shop assistant gave me ____ change today. I bought a book for £2.99, gave her £10 and she gave me £8.01 change instead of £7.01. I don't think she can count.

10. I went for a job interview this afternoon. They said I was ____ old. They want someone under the age of thirty and I am thirty five.

Exercise Twenty One/Answers

1. The bus is crowded. There are **too many** people on it.

2. Person A: "This jumper is **too** small." Person B: "Take it back a get a bigger one."

3. I went to the supermarket to buy some food. It was **too** late. When I got there, it was closed.

4. There were **too many** people in the post office. I didn't have time to wait in the queue so I left.

5. Person A: "This cake is disgusting. Person B: I know. I put **too much** flour in it.

6. Person B: "I think you left it in the oven for **too** long. It's burnt around the edges."

7. I ate **too much** for lunch today so I don't want any dinner. I'm not hungry.

8. That table is **too** big. There is no space in the kitchen. We need to buy a smaller one.

9. The shop assistant gave me **too much** change today. I bought a book for £2.99, gave her £10 and she gave me £8.01 change instead of £7.01. I don't think she can count.

10. I went for a job interview this afternoon. They said I was **too** old. They want someone under the age of thirty and I am thirty five.

Note from the author:

Always try to remember that we use too +adjective, too much + uncountable noun and too many + countable noun

Exercise Twenty Two

Enough

The word '**enough**' is deleted from the following sentences. Put it back into its correct position.

Example:

0. I don't have money to go out tonight.

   I don't have **enough** money to go out tonight.

1. These shoes are not big. They're too small.
2. I can't see the football match. I'm not tall.
3. Do you know English to hold a conversation?
4. She saved money to buy a car.
5. This tea is not hot. Add some more hot water to it. I don't like tepid tea.
6. I cooked food for ten people last night but only four guests came to the dinner party. I now have food and drink to last all week. (enough x 2)
7. The new house is not big for guests. It only has a one bedroom.
8. Hurry up! We're late. We don't have time to have breakfast.
9. There's not hot water to have a bath. Linda used most of it to wash her hair.
10. There's not light in this room. I can't see where I'm going. It's too dark.

Exercise Twenty Two/Answers

1. These shoes are not big **enough**. They're too small.

2. I can't see the football match. I'm not tall **enough**.

3. Do you know **enough** English to hold a conversation?

4. She saved **enough** money to buy a car.

5. This tea is not hot **enough**. Add some more hot water to it. I don't like tepid tea.

6. I cooked **enough** food for ten people last night but only four guests came to the dinner party. I now have **enough** food and drink to last all week.

7. The new house is not big **enough** for guests. It only has a one bedroom.

8. Hurry up! We're late. We don't have **enough** time to have breakfast.

9. There's not **enough** hot water to have a bath. Linda used most of it to wash her hair.

10. There's not **enough** light in this room. I can't see where I'm going. It's too dark.

Note from the author:

noun + **enough - enough** adjective

Exercise Twenty Three

A little and A Few

Fill the spaces below with one of the quantifiers "a few" or "a little".

Example:

0. I only have ____ pounds left in my bank account

Answer: I only have **a few** pounds left in my bank account

1. Person A:"Would you like some milk in your tea?"

   Person B: "Just ____ please."

2. ____ of my friends came for dinner last night.

3. On the telephone: "Can I speak to Mark please?"

   "Sorry but he went out ____ minutes ago."

4. Person A: "Dinner is ready. How much rice do you want?"

   Person B: "Just ____ ,I'm not hungry this evening."

5. I need to buy more milk when I go to the supermarket. There is only ____ left from yesterday. It is not enough for our breakfast tomorrow morning.

6. I bought some more oranges because there were only ____ left.

7. There were only ____ people in the queue at the supermarket.

8. Person A: "Did you eat all the biscuits? There are none left."

   Person B: "I didn't eat them all. I only ate ____ .

9. Person A: "This pasta is too salty. How much salt did you put in the water?"

   Person B: "Only ____ ."

10. I found ____ old photographs in the attic this morning. I went up to look for my old boots.

EXERCISE TWENTY THREE/ANSWERS

Fill the spaces below with one of the quantifiers “a few” or “a little”.

Example:

1. Person A:”Would you like some milk in your tea?”

   Person B: “Just **a little** please.”

2. **A few** of my friends came for dinner last night.

3. On the telephone: “Can I speak to Mark please?”

   “Sorry but he went out **a few** minutes ago.”

4. Person A: “Dinner is ready. How much rice do you want?”

   Person B: “Just **a little** .I’m not hungry this evening.”

5. I need to buy more milk when I go to the supermarket. There is only **a little** left from yesterday. It is not enough for our breakfast tomorrow morning.

6. I bought some more oranges because there were only **a few** left.

7. There were only **a few** people in the queue at the supermarket.

8. Person A: “Did you eat all the biscuits? There are none left.”

   Person B: “I didn’t eat them all. I only ate **a few**.

9. Person A: “This pasta is too salty. How much salt did you put in the water?”

   Person B: “Only **a little**.”

10. I found **a few** old photographs in the attic this morning. I went up to look for my old boots.

Note from the author:

“A little” and “ A few” are used to describe a small quantity of something.

We use “a little” + uncountable noun

We use “a few” + countable noun

When the noun is countable, then it is always in the plural form with “ a few” and it is important that the verb is in the plural too.

Example:

A few boys were in the park.

When the noun is uncountable, then it is always in the singular form (with no “s”) when we use “ a little” so it is important that the verb is in the singular form too.

Example:

There is a little orange juice in the glass.

EXERCISE TWENTY FOUR

Fill the gaps with _too/too much/too many/too few/too little/enough/not enough_

Example:

0. There are ____ people in the car. There's ____ space for them all.

Answer: There are **too many** people in the car. There's **not enough** space for them all.

1. There weren't ____ sandwiches for everyone because ____ people came to the opening of the new shop..

2. I've got____ time on my hands since I left my job and I don't have____ money to pay the rent.

3. Person A: "Is your new flat big?" Person B: "It's big ____ for me, but ____ for two. It has only one room."

4. ____ members of parliament agreed on the new law.

5. When we were in London, we didn't have ____ time to see Buckingham Palace. There was ____ time to do much. Two days was not ____ .

6. The problem is that there are____ fishermen trying to catch ____ fish.

7. This tea is ____ sweet. You put ____ sugar in it.

8. There are ____ jobs for ____ people.

9. ____ money is not good for anyone.

10. She's ____ thin. She lost ____ weight when she was in hospital. She didn't eat ____ .

EXERCISE TWENTY FOUR/ANSWERS

1. There weren't **enough** sandwiches for everyone because **too many** people came to the opening of the new shop..

2. I've got **too much** time on my hands since I left my job and I don't have **enough** money to pay the rent.

3. Person A: "Is your new flat big?" Person B: "It's big **enough** for me.

4. **Too few** members of parliament agreed on the new law.

5. When we were in London, we didn't have **enough** time to see Buckingham Palace. There was **not enough** time to do much.

6. The problem is that there are **too many** fishermen trying to catch **too few** fish.

7. This tea is **too** sweet. You put **too much** sugar in it.

8. There are **too few** jobs for **too many** people.

9. **Too much** money is not good for anyone.

10. She's **too** thin. She lost **too much** weight when she was in hospital. She didn't eat **enough**.

Exercise Twenty Five

Vocabulary Quiz Time/Test Your Vocabulary/Numbers

Example:

0. It's the first number

Answer: One (1)

1. A pair or a couple,
2. There are ____ days in a week.
3. A trio.
4. Two plus two (2+2) = ____
5. Your hands have ____ fingers.
6. Three times three (3x3) = ____
7. If you double three, what do you get?
8. If you double four, what do you get?
9. A century is a period of ____ years.
10. There are ____ hours in a day.
11. ____ months make a year.
12. There are ____ of these in a minute.
13. You celebrate your silver wedding anniversary after ____ years.
14. Your golden wedding anniversary is after how many years?
15. The age when you begin to be a teenager.
16. The last age of your teenage years.

17. The age when you can legally drive a car, go to most pubs and do what you want without your parents' consent.

18. This number is similar to two fat women.

19. This number is similar to a pair of legs.

20. This number is similar to two ducks.

Exercise Twenty Five/Answers

1. Two (2)
2. Seven (7)
3. Three (3)
4. Four (4)
5. Ten (10)
6. Nine (9)
7. Six (6)
8. Eight (8)
9. One hundred (100)
10. Twenty four (24)
11. Twelve (12)
12. Sixty (60)
13. Twenty five (25)
14. Fifty (50)
15. Thirteen (13)
16. Nineteen (19)
17. Eighteen (18)
18. Eighty eight (88)
19. Eleven (11)
20. Twenty two (22)

Exercise Twenty Six

Vocabulary Quiz Time/Test Your Vocabulary/Colours

Example: 0. The sky is this colour

Answer: Blue

1. It's the colour of grass.
2. Bananas are this colour.
3. What colour is milk?
4. The colours of a zebra.
5. The colour of blood.
6. Lemons are this colour.
7. Plums can be yellow, red or_____.
8. Your tongue and gums are this colour.
9. The colour of an orange.
10. This colour is darker than white.

Exercise Twenty Six/Answers

1. Green 2. Yellow

3. White 4. Black and white

5. Red 6. Lemon

7. Purple 8. Pink

9. Orange 10. Beige

EXERCISE TWENTY SEVEN

VOCABULARY QUIZ TIME/TEST YOUR VOCABULARY/BASIC BODY

Example:

0. You have two of these on your face and you use them to see.

Answer: **eyes**

1. You have two of these on each side of your head. You use them to hear with or to listen to someone or something.

2. You have one of these on your face. You use it to smell things.

3. You have two of these on your face below number (0). They become pink when you feel embarrassed or if you run.

4. You have this on your head. It can be long, short, curly, wavy or straight. People have different colours of this. Some blonde, some red, some brown and some black.

5. You have five of these on each hand. You need them to write with.

6. You have two of these. You wear shoes on them when you go out.

7. You have five of these on each of number (6).

8. You have two of these. They are attached to your hands and shoulders.

9. The bottom part of your face.

10. The top part of your face.

11. You have two of these and they are attached to number 6.

12. You have many of these. They are white and we use them to eat.

13. Women wear lipstick on these.

14. Women wear nail varnish on these.

15. This joins the shoulders to the head. When it's cold we wear a scarf around it.

16. This is inside our mouths. We need it to taste food.

17. We have two of these on number (2). They are similar to two holes.

18. The part of the body that we sit down on.

19. The part of the body that is above number (18).

20. Where our food goes.

EXERCISE TWENTY SEVEN/ANSWERS

1. Ears	2. Nose	3. Cheeks	4. Hair
5. Fingers	6. Feet/one foot/two feet – irregular plural		
7. Toes	8. Arms	9. Chin	10. Forehead
11. Legs	12. Teeth/one tooth/two teeth – irregular plural		
13. Lips	14. Nails	15. Neck	16. Tongue
17. Nostrils	18. The bottom	19. The back	20. Stomach

EXERCISE TWENTY EIGHT

VOCABULARY QUIZ TIME/TEST YOUR FOOD VOCABULARY

Example:

0. It's a fruit that monkeys like.

Answer: Banana

1. It's a fruit. It can be red, yellow or green. New York is also called the same as this fruit. 'The Big _____'.

2. This fruit comes from hot places such as Sicily or Valencia. It has the same name as its colour. You can eat this fruit or drink it.

3. English people eat this on toast for breakfast in the morning. It's a dairy product.

4. When I make a cup of coffee, I add milk and _____.

5. These are red and often people eat them with salad. Italian people use them to make sauce to put on pasta.

6. A popular cold meat that rhymes with jam.

7. This lovely cheese comes from Italy. We use it on pasta or minestrone.

8. It comes from the bee and is sweet.

9. What do we normally buy when we go to the bakery? We put Number (8). on this and eat it. We also use it to make sandwiches.

10. They are oval. They come from the hen. We can use them in many ways especially for a typical English breakfast with bacon, tomatoes, sausages and _____.

11. We have these with a cup of tea or a cup of coffee. They are round, hard and sweet. Sometimes they are square or rectangular. The Americans call them cookies, but in Britain they have a different name.

12. What you eat when it is your birthday. You put candles on this.

13. We use them to make chips or if you are in America, French fries.

14. A vegetable that rabbits eat.

15. A small round green vegetable.

16. This food comes from the sea.

17. They are small, red and sweet. They grow on trees.

18. A vegetable that ends with the word 'flower'.

19. This vegetable is green. Popeye ate a lot of it to become strong.

20. This fruit is red. Many people eat it with fresh cream. The Beatles sang a song entitled '...... fields forever.'

Exercise Twenty Eight/Answers

1. Apple
2. Orange
3. Butter
4. Sugar
5. Tomatoes
6. Ham
7. Parmesan cheese
8. Honey
9. Bread
10. Eggs
11. Biscuits 'biskits/
12. Cake
13. Potatoes
14. Carrot
15. Pea
16. Fish
17. Cherries
18. Cauliflower
19. Spinach
20. Strawberries

Exercise Twenty Nine

Vocabulary Quiz Time/Test Your Vocabulary/Clothes And Accessories

Example:

0. You put these on your feet before you put on your shoes.

Answer: **Socks**

1. You wear these on your legs. They can be long or they can be short.

2. This has got short sleeves and is usually made of cotton. It takes its name from its shape.

3. This is usually made of wool. It has got long sleeves and you wear it in winter to keep you warm. It can have a round neck, a V-neck, a turtle neck or a polo neck.

4. Businessmen wear these or any male on a formal occasion. You wear them with a tie. They are usually difficult to iron. The most popular colours are white and light blue.

5. We wear these on our feet. They cover your legs too. They are good for the winter months.

6. Soft shoes we wear in the house.

7. You wear these to go to bed.

8. It is something you wear around your neck to keep it warm in winter. It is normally made of wool.

9. You wear these on your hands when it is very cold.

10. You wear these in your ear lobes.

11. It is something you wear on your wrist that tells you the time.

12. This is like a long jacket. You wear it when it is really cold.

13. You wear this on your head. The people in Moscow always wear one.

14. This is similar to number 3. only it has buttons up the front.

15. Women wear this. It can be long, short, or knee-length.

16. You wear these with number 15. They cover your legs and can be made of nylon or wool. In the summer you usually don't need to wear them unless your legs are very white.

17. You wear this with number 1. It is long and usually made of leather. It has a buckle.

18. Women wear this on the beach. It has two pieces.

19. You wear these to protect your eyes when you go out in the sun.

20. These are made of denim and are usually blue. Nearly everyone has a pair.

Exercise Twenty Nine/Answers

1. Trousers
2. T-shirt
3. Jumper
4. Shirt
5. Boots.
6. Slippers
7. Pyjamas
8. A scarf
9. Gloves
10. Earrings
11. A watch
12. A coat
13. A hat
14. A cardigan
15. A skirt
16. Tights
17. A belt
18. A bikini
19. Sunglasses
20. Jeans

Exercise Thirty

Vocabulary Quiz Time/Test Your Vocabulary/Home And Furniture

Example:

0. You sleep on this.

Answer: **A bed**

1. You rest your head on this when you go to sleep at night.

2. A cover you use to keep warm when you go to sleep.

3. It is large and is usually made of wood. It has doors. You keep your clothes in it.

4. You keep your bedside lamp on top of this.

5. These things hang from the windows and keep the light out.

6. Every room in the house has one of these which you open to enter and exit.

7. The top part of a room.

8. Each room has four of these.

9. The part of a house which you walk on.

10. Every kitchen has one of these. It's cool inside and it keeps food fresh.

11. You sit on this.

12. You sit at this to eat.

13. You keep your groceries in this; e.g. sugar, coffee, tea etc.

14. Two things you need to use to cut and eat meat.

15. You use this to put sugar in your tea and to stir it.

16. You use this to eat cereal or soup.

17. You drink your tea or coffee from this.

18. You use this to drink milk, water or any other cold drink from.

19. You put your lunch or dinner on this then you eat from it.

20. You cook roast beef, roast chicken and roast potatoes in this.

21. You use this to fry food in.

22. You use this to cook pasta in.

23. You use this to heat the water for the pasta. You need to light it first.

24. The name we give to the whole machine we use to cook our food.

25. It's what we use to cut bread.

27. Many homes have these on their walls.

28. Where we keep our books.

29. It's something you open and put things in. For example: socks and underwear and other things.

30. We relax on this in front of the TV. Normally it has room for two or three people.

31. These are square shaped and soft. We usually have them on Number 30..

32. It's something you sit in to relax. It is similar to number 30. but it is only for one person. It has arms on it.

33. We use this to dry our faces or hands or our body. We keep it in the bathroom.

34. It's a machine that we use to wash our clothes in.

35. It's in the bathroom. We fill this with hot water and then get into it and lie back and relax. Many people put bubble bath in this before they get into it.

36. It's a place in the bathroom where you get washed but it is different from number 35. because you need to stand up.

37. When you get out of number 36., you put this on you to dry yourself. It is similar to number 33. but it is bigger. It also has a hood, pockets and sleeves on it.

38. It's in the bathroom and we wash our hands and faces in it.

39. Water comes out of these.

40. This is in the kitchen. It is similar to number 38. but we use it to wash dishes by hand.

Exercise Thirty/Answers

1. A pillow 2. A blanket

3. A wardrobe 4. Bedside table/bedside cabinet

5. Curtains 6. A door

7. The ceiling 8. Walls

9. The floor 10. A fridge

11. A chair 12. A table

13. Kitchen cupboards/kitchen cabinets

14. A knife and fork 15. A teaspoon

16. A spoon 17. A cup

18. A glass 19. A plate

20. An oven 21. A frying pan

22. A pot 23. A gas ring or an electric ring

24. A cooker 25. A bread knife

27. Pictures or paintings

28. On a bookshelf or in a bookcase

29. Drawers

30. A sofa or a couch or a settee there are three names for this.

31. Cushions 32. An armchair

33. A towel 34. A washing machine.

35. A bath 36. A shower

37. A bathrobe 38. A wash basin

39. Taps 40. A sink

The End

Printed in Germany
by Amazon Distribution
GmbH, Leipzig